Learning to Read, Step by Step!

Ready to Read Preschool–Kindergarten
• big type and easy words • rhyme and rhythm • picture clues
For children who know the alphabet and are eager to begin reading.

Reading with Help Preschool–Grade 1
• basic vocabulary • short sentences • simple stories
For children who recognize familiar words and sound out new words with help.

Reading on Your Own Grades 1–3
• engaging characters • easy-to-follow plots • popular topics
For children who are ready to read on their own.

Reading Paragraphs Grades 2–3
• challenging vocabulary • short paragraphs • exciting stories
For newly independent readers who read simple sentences with confidence.

Ready for Chapters Grades 2–4
• chapters • longer paragraphs • full-color art
For children who want to take the plunge into chapter books but still like colorful pictures.

STEP INTO READING® is designed to give every child a successful reading experience. The grade levels are only guides; children will progress through the steps at their own speed, developing confidence in their reading. The F&P Text Level on the back cover serves as another tool to help you choose the right book for your child.

Remember, a lifetime love of reading starts with a single step!

For Adelaide Alberto—a girl with a book
—S.C.

For Malala!
—E.S.

Text copyright © 2016 by Shana Corey
Illustrations copyright © 2016 by Elizabeth Sayles
Photograph credits: Cover: © European Union—European Parliament, Pietro Naj-Oleari, 2013; p. 21: courtesy of Fazal Khaliq; p. 31: courtesy of Myra Iqbal; pp. 44–45: Official White House photo by Pete Souza; p. 47: Nigel Waldron/Getty Images Entertainment/Getty Images

Visit us on the Web!
StepIntoReading.com
randomhousekids.com

Educators and librarians, for a variety of teaching tools, visit us at RHTeachersLibrarians.com

Library of Congress Cataloging-in-Publication Data
Corey, Shana.
Malala : a hero for all / by Shana Corey ; illustrations by Elizabeth Sayles.
pages cm. — (Step into reading, step 4)
ISBN 978-0-553-53761-1 (trade pbk.) — ISBN 978-0-553-53762-8 (lib. bdg.) — ISBN 978-0-553-53763-5 (ebook)
1. Yousafzai, Malala, 1997– —Juvenile literature. 2. Girls—Education—Pakistan—Juvenile literature. 3. Pakistan—Social conditions—Juvenile literature. I. Title.
LC2330.C67 2016 371.822095491—dc23 2014047751

Printed in the United States of America
10 9 8 7 6 5 4 3 2

This book has been officially leveled by using the F&P Text Level Gradient™ Leveling System.

Malala
A Hero for All

by Shana Corey

illustrations by Elizabeth Sayles

Random House New York

Chapter 1
The Power of Words

A young girl stands at a podium. Today is her birthday. She is sixteen years old. But she is not celebrating with an ordinary party and cake. Instead, she is in front of an audience at the United Nations in New York City.

Hundreds of people wait to hear what she will say. She looks out at the crowd. Then she begins to speak.

She talks about peace. She talks about children's right to an education. "It's time to speak up," she says. "Our words can change the world."

When she is finished, the audience
rises and gives her a standing ovation.
The young girl in front of them is a hero.

Chapter 2
A Baby Is Born

On July 12, 1997, a tiny baby came kicking and screaming into the world. If the baby had been a boy, guns would have been fired in celebration. Gifts would have been piled into the baby's cradle. The baby's name would have been written in the family tree.

But this baby was a girl. In the country of Pakistan, a girl's birth is usually not considered a reason to celebrate. It's not even worth writing down.

This baby's parents were different, though. They named the new baby Malala, after Malalai, a famous heroine who had inspired an army with her words.

Malala Yousafzai's father was a teacher and a poet and the principal of a school. He wrote her name on the family tree next to the boys and men who had come before her. And he taught her the story of Malalai.

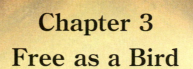

Chapter 3
Free as a Bird

Malala and her family are members of the Pashtun people. During her childhood, they lived in the city of Mingora, which is in the Swat Valley in Pakistan.

Malala loved her valley. There were beautiful mountains and sparkling waterfalls. In the summer, wildflowers turned the fields into a rainbow, and ripe pomegranates, peaches, and figs filled the trees.

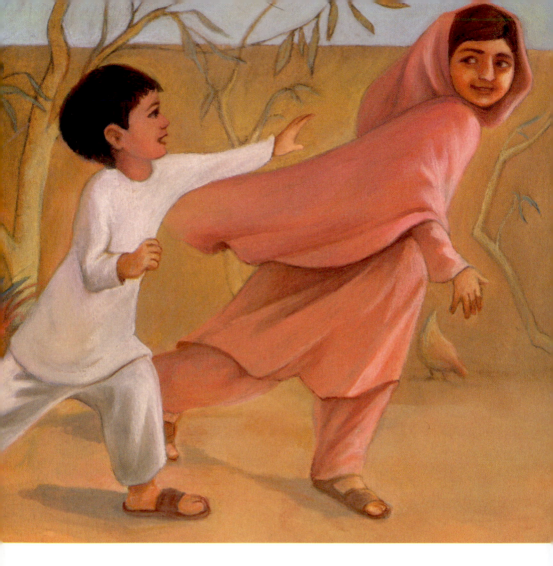

In many ways, Malala was a regular Pashtun girl. She loved pizza and cupcakes, and hated eggplant.

She played cricket and tag and hide-and-seek. She had picnics in the summer and built snowmen in the winter.

She shared secrets with her best friend, Moniba, and fought with her two younger brothers.

And she sat on her rooftop and dreamed.

Malala's favorite television show was about a boy with a magic pencil. The boy could make anything he wanted with his pencil. Malala wished *she* had a magic pencil!

In other ways, Malala was *not* an ordinary Pashtun girl.

In Pakistan, boys and girls were not considered equal.

Older girls weren't supposed to leave their house unless they had a male relative with them. They weren't even allowed to look men in the eye.

Most Pashtun women followed the code of "purdah," which meant they covered themselves—including their faces—when they were in public.

Malala said she would never cover her face. And to everyone's surprise, her father agreed. "Malala will live as free as a bird," he said.

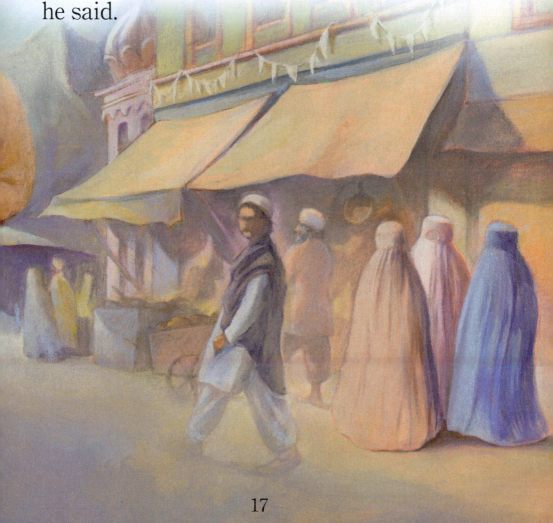

Chapter 4
Education

Malala adored her father. Their house was often filled with visitors. While the other women and girls cooked and chatted, Malala liked to sit with her father and listen to the men talk about politics and the world.

Education wasn't considered important for girls in Pakistan. Many girls stopped going to school by age ten, if they were able to go at all. And many girls and women—including Malala's own mother—did not know how to read.

But Malala's father believed that education should be for everyone—including girls.

With his stories and songs, Malala's father taught her the power of words.

When she was just a toddler, he'd bring her to school with him. She'd stand in front of an empty classroom and pretend to be a teacher. Sometimes she'd listen to a real teacher instruct the older children.

And when she was almost five, her father enrolled her in school.

Malala loved school! Every year, the children competed to get the prize for being the top student. Malala usually won. She was very proud, and *very* competitive.

Chapter 5
A Magic Pencil

Malala's mother taught her about helping others. She cooked extra food to give to poor families. She invited children who didn't have enough food at home to come over for breakfast before school.

Malala's family had known what it was like to be hungry, and her mother taught her to share what they had now.

One day, Malala's mother sent her to the dump to throw out some potato peels and eggshells.

The air smelled of garbage. Flies buzzed overhead. And rats scurried through the filth. Malala walked carefully, trying not to spoil her shoes.

Suddenly, she saw something move.

To her surprise, it was a girl. The girl was sorting trash into piles. Nearby, other children searched through the trash for bits of metal.

When she asked her father about those children, he explained that they were looking for things they could sell to help support their families.

Malala couldn't stop thinking about those children. She wished once more that she had a magic pencil so she could use it to help them.

But she didn't have a magic pencil. And she realized she couldn't wait for someone else to do something. If she wanted the world to change, she would have to change it. "Why should I wait for someone else?" she said later. "Why don't I raise my voice?"

So she took her real pencil and wrote a letter to God. She asked for the courage to make the world better.

She tied her letter to a piece of wood and placed a dandelion on top. Then she floated it down the stream that flowed into the Swat River and hoped that God would find it.

Chapter 6
The Taliban

When Malala was around eight years old, a mullah (a kind of religious leader) started a radio station. The mullah said music and movies and television should be outlawed. He said women should go out only in emergencies. He said girls' schools should be outlawed as well.

The "Radio Mullah" grew more and more popular.

He joined forces with the Taliban, a powerful group that began in the nearby country of Afghanistan. The Taliban believed women should not be educated.

They used violence and fear to get their way. They burned down girls' schools. They made it illegal for women to go shopping. The Taliban beat people—and sometimes killed them—if they didn't follow these extreme rules.

Malala's family hid their television in the closet. But they didn't back down.

Her father kept his school open. Malala admired his bravery. Still, she was scared.

Pakistan's army came to the Swat Valley to fight the Taliban. At night, the house shook and the skies were bright with bombs.

But during the day, Malala and her classmates studied and debated and learned.

"We will continue our education," said Malala.

In January 2009, the Taliban declared that all girls' schools must close by January 15.

Fewer and fewer girls came to class now. Many teachers quit. People were afraid.

Malala's father had a friend who worked for the British Broadcasting Corporation (BBC). The friend asked her father if one of his students would write about life under the Taliban.

Malala was only eleven years old. But she had watched her father speak out about girls' right to an education. She'd read books about activists like Martin Luther King Jr., and Meena—a woman who had fought for women's rights in Afghanistan. She knew she couldn't wait for someone else to speak up for her.

Maybe she had a kind of magic pencil after all.

Chapter 7
One Voice

And so Malala began to write a blog.

"I am afraid," she wrote in her first entry.

She wrote about schools being destroyed, about violence in the streets. And about how sad she was when she couldn't go to school.

Malala's words traveled outside Mingora, outside the Swat Valley, and even outside Pakistan.

People all over the world read about the Pakistani schoolgirl who was fighting for her right to an education.

Malala's words reached a reporter for the *New York Times*. He came to interview her for a film.

"They cannot stop me. I will get my education, if it is in home, school, or anyplace," she said.

The violence continued. Malala went to school in secret. She didn't wear her uniform. She hid her books under her shawl.

And she continued to speak out every chance she got.

"The girls of Swat are not afraid of anyone," she said bravely.

The Taliban had threatened Malala's father before. Now they threatened her. But she would not stop speaking out against them.

On October 9, 2012, Malala was fifteen years old. She took her exams as usual that day. Then she headed home on the school bus, Moniba sitting beside her.

That was the last thing she would remember from that day.

Chapter 8
Thousands of Voices

Malala woke up a week later in a hospital. She was thousands of miles from home, and she didn't know what had happened.

She learned that the Taliban had shot her in the side of the head. Somehow she had survived. She had been airlifted to a hospital in England.

The Taliban had tried to silence Malala. But they had failed.

Reporters told Malala's story. People from all over the world said prayers and sent letters and cards. Children, movie stars, and world leaders wished Malala a speedy recovery.

People protested against the Taliban
and told the world they stood with Malala.
Over two million people signed the
Right to Education petition.

Malala recovered and moved to a new home in England with her family. She attended a new school. But Malala's fight for girls' education wasn't over.

Millions of girls still aren't able to go to school. Malala travels the world

speaking about girls' education. She
has met the queen of England and the
president of the United States.

She created the Malala Fund to help
girls everywhere get food, shelter, and
an education.

On Malala's sixteenth birthday, the whole world celebrated Malala Day. The girl whose name wasn't supposed to be worth writing down gave a speech before the United Nations. Children from over ninety countries filled the audience. Millions of people watched at home.

"We realize the importance of our voice when we are silenced," she said. "One child, one teacher, one pen, and one book can change the world."

Malala was right. She had spoken up and people had heard her.

In 2014, at the age of seventeen, she became the youngest person ever to win the Nobel Peace Prize.

Malala's voice, her willingness to take a stand, *had* changed the world.

Author's Note

The quotations in this book are from Malala's speeches, interviews, and blog. Most of them come from her speech to the United Nations on July 12, 2013. You can watch the speech—ask an adult to help you find the video online.

How Can You Help?

Go to Malala.org or AWorldAtSchool.org to find out how you can help girls across the globe get access to education.

And if you're ready for more, you can read Malala's autobiography, *I Am Malala: The Young Readers Edition* (Little, Brown, 2014).